Try out these amazing samosa recipes and serve them as appetizers or an evening snack over tea. You can also make dozens at a time and freeze them for weeks up to a month and use whenever you crave a samosa or have unexpected guests coming over.

Happy Eating!

CW01499209

TABLE OF CONTENTS

The Samosa Cookbook

30 Crispy and Crunchy Samosa Recipes

Bobby Flatt

INTRODUCTION

The samosa is a fairly popular street food all over India and even in Pakistan. If you enjoy Indian cuisine then you are definitely familiar with the samosa and its types. These are crunchy and crispy bites stuffed with varied filling and are mostly deep fried. They are served with various chutneys and sauces, for example, raita (seasoned yogurt), red chili chutney, mint chutney, sweet tamarind chutney and tomato sauce.

Cooking samosa is relatively easy. There are some basic ingredients that form the base of its cooking. The main condiment of a samosa is its shell. The main ingredients for making pastry dough are flour, Coram seeds, salt, ghee and water. No matter what kind of samosa you are making these ingredients are the foundation of making the pastry.

This samosa cookbook features 30 different recipes of samosas. These recipes are not only easy to make but the samosa fillings are also very basic and delicious. You can have so much creativity with the filling ingredients. You can also use your leftovers as stuffing and a whole new snack is ready in no time.

If you are a beginner then making pastry and shaping it will be a little daunting for you but once you get a hold of the trick, you will be able to make dozens of these pastries in half the time. Samosa sheets are also easily available in the market. They are known by different names which are, samosa strips, samosa patties and samosa rolls. However, there's no difference between any of them.

KEEMA SAMOSA

This crispy samosa recipe contains beef mince filling. These are deep fried to give a crunchy texture. The trick to an aromatic and delicious filling is to cook it until the meat has dried completely. In addition do not cook the onions with the meat for too long to avoid sogginess.

Servings: 12

Preparation Time: 30 minutes

INGREDIENTS:

For the filling:
- Minced beef meat, 1 kg
- Onions, 1 cup, chopped
- Garlic paste, 1 teaspoon
- Turmeric powder, 1 teaspoon
- Butter, 1 tablespoon
- Lemon juice, 1
- Garam masala, 1 teaspoon
- Ginger paste, 1 teaspoon
- Coriander, 1 bunch, chopped
- Salt, to taste
- Green chilies, 3, chopped
- Cumin powder, 1 tablespoon
- Ground cumin, 2 tablespoon

For the dough:
- Wheat flour, ¾ cup
- Salt, ¼ teaspoon
- Lukewarm water, ¼ cup
- Oil, ½ tablespoon

METHOD:

1. Mix beef meat with garlic, ginger, allspices, chilies, half of coriander, salt and half of lemon juice. Cook the meat in a pan on medium-high flame until it dries. Stir frequently.
2. When the meat dries completely add onions and mix well. Turn the flame low and add turmeric. Cook for 3 minutes and combine well.
3. Remove from the flame.
4. Add remaining spices, butter and lemon juice. Combine everything well.

5. To make dough combine all the dough ingredients together except for water.
6. Add water gradually and knead to make firm dough.
7. Let the dough stand for 15 minutes.
8. Split the dough into 4 pieces and roll each piece between your palms. Further slice each piece into half and make semicircles. Fold the dough into a cone shape and stuff it with the meat filling. Apply water on the edges so that the cone does not open.
9. Deep fry the samosas until nicely golden. Serve immediately.

CHEESE SAMOSA

Cheese samosas are very unique and unusual in taste. This recipe uses packaged samosa strips but you can also use spring roll strips; just divide them in three parts. Make sure you fry the samosas when the oil has reached the right temperature. You don't want to burn your samosas.

Servings: 10

Preparation Time: 20 minutes

INGREDIENTS:

- Samosa strips, 10
- Onion, 1 large, chopped
- Black pepper, 1 pinch
- Oregano, ½ teaspoon
- Green chili, 1, chopped
- Cream cheese, 100 g

METHOD:

1. Combine all the spices with cream cheese.
2. Taste and add more spices if you want. Remember cheese samosa's are not too spicy but very moderate.
3. Take one end of the samosa sheet and fold it to form a triangle. Fold it again in the same direction and you will get a cone shape.
4. Stuff the cone with mixture and fold the remaining edges together in the same triangular direction.
5. Apply some water to bind the edges together.
6. Deep fry until golden brown.
7. Serve immediately.

MAWA SAMOSA

This is a traditional Indian sweet treat made with mawa and combined with raisins, cashews and cardamom. The batter is made with milk and sugar for extra sweetness. These are perfect sweet bites when craving something traditional.

Servings: 6

Preparation Time: 15 minutes

INGREDIENTS:

For the dough:
- Plain flour, 2 cups
- Ghee, 2.5 tablespoon
- Milk, 3 tablespoon
- Sugar, ½ cup

For filling:
- Mawa, ½ kg
- Castor sugar, 4 tablespoons
- Raisins, 3 tablespoons
- Cashew nuts, 3 tablespoons, chopped
- Green cardamom, 5, grounded

METHOD:

1. Combine flour with sugar. Apply ghee on your fingertips and start mixing the flour mixture.
2. Gradually pour milk and knead to make a firm and smooth dough.
3. Split the dough into 10 pieces and roll between your palms to make balls.
4. Halve each ball and spread to make strips. Keep aside while you prepare the filling.
5. Mix mawa and milk together and add cardamom, raisins, sugar and cashews. Combine well.
6. Stuff each dough strip with the filling and apply water on the edges to bind well.
7. Deep fry until golden.
8. Serve immediately.

MUSHROOM SAMOSA

This recipe uses mushroom and soy chunks filling in the samosa. These samosas are easy to make but the process of making dough can be a little daunting. This recipe makes enough samosas for you to refrigerate for weeks.

Servings:	60 samosas
Preparation Time:	30 minutes

INGREDIENTS:

- Mushrooms, 350 g
- Curry leaves, 1 sprig, chopped
- Turmeric powder, ½ teaspoon
- Salt, 1 ¼ teaspoon
- Soy chunks, 200 g, soaked in water for 30 minutes
- Tomato. 100 g, chopped
- Hot green chilies, 4. chopped
- Eggs, 4
- Hot red chili powder, 1 ½ teaspoons
- Onions, 250 g, chopped
- Garam masala, 1 teaspoon
- Black pepper, ½ teaspoon

For dough:
- Wheat flour, 750 g
- Water
- Salt, 1 teaspoon
- Gingerly seeds, 2 teaspoons
- Coconut oil, 2 tablespoons

METHOD:

1. Chop mushrooms and soy chunks. Season with salt, turmeric, garam masala and red chili powder. Combine well and keep aside.
2. Stir fry onions, curry leaves and green chilies. When the onions turns brown add tomatoes and cook for 2 minutes while stirring continuously.
3. Add mushrooms and soy chunks. Combine everything together and cover the lid of the pan. Cook for 15 minutes.
4. Meanwhile beat eggs. After 15 minutes add egg mixture slowly while stirring continuously on high flame.

5. When everything is well incorporated season with black pepper and remove from flame.
6. To prepare dough, combine all the dough ingredients together and knead to form stiff dough.
7. Take small portions of the dough and roll it between your palms. Flatten the rolled dough and cut it into halve.
8. Take one piece of the halved dough turn one end over the other and overlap the edges making cone shape.
9. Stuff the cones with the mushroom mixture and fold the remaining edges together. Apply a little water for binding.
10. Deep fry until very light golden.
11. Serve immediately.

SCRAMBLED TOFU SAMOSA

If you like tofu then this scrambled tofu samosa recipe is a must try. These samosas have a simple filling and require little time to assemble. These can also be baked if you are watching your weight.

Servings: 6-8

Preparation Time: 30 minutes

INGREDIENTS:

For the filling:
- Scrambled tofu, 1 cup

For dough:
- All-purpose flour, ½ cup
- Whole wheat flour, ½ cup
- Carom seeds, ½ teaspoon, crushed
- Yogurt, ½ cup
- Oil, 1 tablespoon
- Salt, to taste
- Red chili powder, to taste

METHOD:

1. Combine the dry ingredients of dough together. Apply some oil on your fingertips and rub the mixture to combine well.
2. Add water and yogurt and start kneading to form stiff dough. Keep aside for 15 minutes.
3. After 15 minutes divide the dough into half.
4. Take small portion of the dough and roll them between your palms. Flatten the dough and turn the edges together to make a cone.
5. Fill the cone with tofu filling and seal the open edges.
6. Deep fry until nicely golden.
7. Serve immediately.

FRIED RICE SAMOSA

This recipe is perfect to put leftover fried rice to best use. This recipe uses packaged samosa strips. You can buy a pack of 1 or 2 of these and store them in your pantry. These could come handy at any time.

Servings: 12

Preparation Time: 25 minutes

INGREDIENTS:

- Cooked rice, 2 cups
- Onion, ½ cup, chopped
- Salt, to taste
- Green peas, ¼ cup
- Green chili, 4, chopped
- Carrot, 1, chopped
- Garam masala, 1 teaspoon
- Eggs, 3
- Samosa strips, 12

For tempering:
- Curry leaves, 4-6
- Cumin, 1 teaspoon
- Oil, 2 teaspoon

METHOD:

1. Add oil in a large pan and stir cumin and curry leaves. Temper it for 3-5 minutes.
2. Add onions, carrots, green peas and green chili. Cook until veggies are tender while stirring occasionally. Add garam masala
3. Meanwhile beat eggs in a bowl.
4. Gradually add eggs and keep stirring continuously. Cook for 10 minutes.
5. Add rice and season with salt.
6. Combine everything well.
7. Now take each samosa strip and fold one end to make a cone shape.
8. Fill the cone with rice filling. Apply some water on the open end and overlap it on the cone to bind well.
9. Deep fry until nicely golden.
10. Serve immediately.

CHOCOLATE SAMOSA

Yes, we have a chocolate samosa recipe for you as well. Chocolate can be cooked in various forms and there's so much more to be discovered yet. These sweet and crunchy Choco-samosa bites are served with a chilled creamy cappuccino sauce.

Servings: 16

Preparation Time: 15 minutes

INGREDIENTS:

For filling:
- Dark chocolate, 250 g
- Fresh cream, 1 cup

For dough:
- Plain flour, 2 cups
- Ghee, ½ cup
- Oil

For cappuccino cream sauce:
- Coffee powder, 1 teaspoon
- Sugar, 5 tablespoon
- Fresh cream, 1 cup
- Egg yolk, 1

METHOD:

1. Knead flour with ghee and water. Keep side and cover with a damp cloth.
2. Grate chocolate and combine it well with cream. Refrigerate until chilled.
3. Split the dough into 7 pieces and roll each piece in an oval shape. Divide it further into half and fold the edges to made cones.
4. Stuff the cones with chocolate and cream stuffing. Apply some water on the open edges and overlap to seal tightly. Refrigerate.
5. Meanwhile prepare cappuccino sauce. Beat egg yolk and sugar together until it becomes fluffy.
6. Heat cream on low-medium flame in a pan. When it starts to simmer, add this in the egg mixture and fold everything together.

7. Transfer the cream mixture back to the same pan and cook on low flame while stirring nonstop.
8. Add coffee powder and stir well. Keep cooking until it reaches a sauce like consistency.
9. Strain and refrigerate to cool down.
10. Deep fry the refrigerated samosas until golden.
11. Serve immediately with cappuccino sauce.

PANEER SAMOSA

These crispy and crunchy samosas are stuffed with paneer and seasoned with spices to give them a spicy kick. You can add carrots and green peas if you like them in the stuffing. Serve them with coriander chutney for extra flavor.

Servings: 8

Preparation Time: 20 minutes

INGREDIENTS:

- Coriander, 2 tablespoon, chopped
- Ginger-green chili paste, 1 teaspoon
- Cumin seeds, ½ teaspoon
- Oil, 1 tablespoon
- Capsicum, ¼ cup, finely chopped
- Paneer, 1 cup, chopped
- Onions, ¼ cup, chopped
- Salt, to taste
- Dried mango powder, 1 ½ teaspoon
- Chili powder, 1 teaspoon
- Samosa strips, 8

METHOD:

1. Temper cumin seeds in oil and add onions and ginger green chili paste.
2. Sauté for 3 minutes. Add mango powder, paneer, capsicum, coriander, salt and chili powder. Combine everything and cook for 5 minutes.
3. When the mixture cools down start assembling.
4. Turn the edge of a samosa strip and form a triangle shape. Fold it again and stuff the filling.
5. Apply a little water on the open edges and overlap to seal.
6. Deep fry the samosas until golden.
7. Serve immediately.

MATAR SOYA SAMOSA

This is a vegan recipe. It is also good for those who are avoiding meat for some time. If you don't like green peas then you can omit them. These samosas will taste equally delicious without the green peas aswell.

Servings: 4-6
Preparation Time: 15 minutes

INGREDIENTS:

- Soy granules, 50 g, soaked in water for 15 minutes
- Coriander powder, 1 teaspoon
- Soy refined oil
- Garlic paste, 2 teaspoon
- Cumin seeds, 1 teaspoon
- Ghee, 2 tablespoon
- Red chili powder, to taste
- Salt, to taste
- Chaat masala, 2 teaspoon
- Ginger paste, 2 teaspoon
- Coram seeds, 1 teaspoon
- Green peas, 1 cup
- Wheat flour, 250 g
- Potatoes, 2, boiled and peeled
- Green chilies, 4, chopped

METHOD:

1. Mash potatoes and keep aside.
2. Combine flour with ghee, salt and Coram and knead into a stiff dough. Keep the dough aside while the filing is cooked. Cover with a damp cloth.
3. Temper cumin seeds in 2 teaspoon of oil. Add all the spices and combine.
4. Add mashed potatoes, green peas and soy. Combine well and cook until done.
5. Take small portions of the dough and roll them between your palms. Flatten the dough and cut it in half.
6. Turn the edges to form a cone and fill the potato-soy mixture. Apply a little water on the edges to bind well.
7. Deep fry in soy oil until crisp and golden.
8. Serve immediately.

PASTA SAMOSA

This recipe can also be made with some leftover pasta from last night's dinner. We often end up making too much pasta, which cannot be finished the same day. So this is the ideal way to put that pasta to good use. Serve these samosas with mint chutney or red chili sauce for added flavor.

Servings: 6

Preparation Time: 20 minutes

INGREDIENTS:

- Marconi, 1 cup, boiled
- Tomato sauce, 2 tablespoon
- Oregano, ¼ teaspoon
- Onion, 1, chopped
- Vinegar, 2 tablespoon
- Olive oil, 2 tablespoon
- White pepper, to taste
- Red chili sauce, 2 tablespoon
- Capsicum, 1, chopped
- Ginger-garlic paste, 1 teaspoon
- Dried red chili, ½ teaspoon, chopped
- Samosa strips, 6

METHOD:

1. Sauté garlic-ginger paste with capsicums in olive oil.
2. Mix macaroni with oregano, tomato sauce, vinegar, red chilies, chili sauce, white pepper and vinegar. Add capsicums and combine well and set aside.
3. Take each samosa strip and make cone shapes. Fill each cone with the filling.
4. Apply some water on the open edges to seal.
5. Deep fry until golden.
6. Serve immediately.

CHOW MEIN SAMOSA

This is another easy recipe to try out for an evening snack. You can add different vegetables of your choice to the noodles. Serve them with tomato sauce or sweet tamarind chutney for extra flavor.

Servings:	4
Preparation Time:	20 minutes

INGREDIENTS:

- Samosa sheets, 4
- Noodles, 1 cup, boiled
- Lemon juice, 1 teaspoon
- Green peas, ¼ teaspoon
- Green chili, 1, chopped
- Carrot, ¼ cup, chopped
- Soy sauce, ½ teaspoon
- Mushrooms, 2, chopped
- Grated ginger, ½ inch piece
- Salt, ¼ teaspoon
- Black pepper, ¼ teaspoon
- Red chili powder, ¼ teaspoon
- Coriander, 2-3 tablespoon

METHOD:

1. Sauté ginger, peas, and green chili for 3 minutes.
2. Add carrots and sauté for an additional 3 minutes.
3. Add mushrooms, lemon juice, red chili powder, salt, soy sauce, and black pepper. Combine well and cook for 2 minutes.
4. Add noodles and coriander. Combine well and cook for 1 minute. Remove from flame.
5. Take each samosa sheet and make a cone by joining the edges and overlapping them.
6. Fill the cone with spoonful noodle mixture.
7. Apply some water on the open edges to seal well.
8. Deep fry until golden.
9. Serve immediately.

FISH SAMOSA

Are you tired of making the same old dishes with fish? How about season it with some spices and coat it with flour-made sheets and deep fry to make crispy and crunchy fish samosas? You can always serveit with tomato sauce or red chili sauce.

Servings: 4-6
Preparation Time: 35 minutes

INGREDIENTS:

- Boneless fish, 1 ½ cup
- Onion, 1 small, chopped
- Garam masala, 1 teaspoon
- Potato, 1, mashed
- Ginger-garlic paste, 1 teaspoon
- Black pepper, ¼ teaspoon
- Salt, to taste
- Chili powder, ½ teaspoon
- Samosa sheets, 4-6

METHOD:

1. Slice fish into tiny pieces.
2. Sauté onions with ginger-garlic paste.
3. Add fish and season with salt, garam masala and chili powder. Combine well and cook for 10-15 minutes.
4. When the fish is cooked, add potatoes and season with pepper. Combine well. And cook for 2 minutes.
5. Take each samosa sheet and make cones. Fill the cones with fish mixture and apply a little water on the open edge to seal.
6. Deep fry until golden.
7. Serve immediately.

JAM SAMOSA

This is another recipe of a sweet samosa that can also be served after your meal as dessert. This recipe uses mixed fruit jam however you can replace it with any flavor of jam you like. Make sure you do moderate stuffing otherwise your samosas will be too sweet to eat.

Photo Credit: Flickr user Brett Jordan,
<https://www.flickr.com/photos/x1brett/11891201963/>

Servings:	12
Preparation Time:	25 minutes

INGREDIENTS:

- Mawa, 400 g
- Raisins, 3 tablespoons
- Mixed fruit jam, 6 tablespoons

For dough:
- Flour, 2 cups
- Milk, ½ cup
- Sugar, ½ cup
- Oil
- Ghee, 2 ½ tablespoon

METHOD:

1. Sieve flour and add sugar. Apply some ghee on fingertips and rub over the mixture to combine. Gradually add milk and knead to form stiff dough.
2. Divide dough into small pieces. Roll each piece and flatten it. Cut it into half and fold the edges to make cones.
3. Stuff the cones with jam, raisins and mawa.
4. Apply a little water on the open edges to seal.
5. Deep fry until golden.
6. Serve immediately.

POTATO AND PEAS SAMOSA

For those of you who are vegan here is a pure vegan samosa recipe. These samosas are stuffed with spicy mashed potatoes and peas. You can adjust the quantity of spices according to your taste. Serve it with red chili sauce or raita.

Servings: 12

Preparation Time: 45 minutes

INGREDIENTS:

- Potatoes, 1 ¼ pound, boiled and mashed
- Mustard seeds, ½ teaspoon
- Garam masala, ¾ teaspoon
- Red Chili powder, ¼ teaspoon
- Peas, 1/3 cup
- Samosa sheets, 12
- Ground coriander, 1 tablespoon
- Ground cumin, 1 teaspoon
- Mango powder, 2 teaspoons
- Butter, 5 tablespoons, melted
- Sesame seeds, 2 tablespoons
- Water
- Ginger, 1 teaspoon, chopped
- Onion, 1/3 cup, chopped
- Coriander leaves, 4 tablespoons, chopped
- Salt, to taste

METHOD:

1. Temper mustard seeds in oil for 15 seconds.
2. Add onion and ginger. Sauté for 5 minutes.
3. Add a little water and add peas, salt, mango powder and remaining seasoning. Cook for 1 minute and combine well.
4. Add potatoes and coriander leaves. Combine well. Cook for 5-7 minutes.
5. Take each samosa sheet and fold the edges to form a cone.
6. Fill each cone with spoonful of the potato mixture. Seal the sheet and deep fry until golden.
7. Serve immediately.

EGG SAMOSA

This is one of the simplest and easiest samosa recipes. The eggs are made in the same way you make scrambled eggs. The seasoning can be adjusted according to your taste.

Servings: 20

Preparation Time: 15 minutes

INGREDIENTS:

- Eggs, 3 large
- Red chili powder, 1 teaspoon
- Onions, 2, chopped
- Mint leaves, ¼ cup, chopped
- Salt, to taste
- Coriander leaves, ½ cup

METHOD:

1. Whisk eggs until fluffy and wobbly.
2. Pulse all the remaining ingredients together in a food processor and form a paste.
3. Add this paste in eggs mixture while whisking constantly.
4. Heat oil in a pan and pour the egg mixture. Keep stirring to scramble the eggs. Cook thoroughly.
5. Take each samosa sheet and fold the edges to make a cone shape.
6. Stuff each cone with spoonful of egg mixture. Apply a little water on the open edges to bind.
7. Deep fry until golden.
8. Serve immediately.

DILL LEAVES SWEET POTATO SAMOSA

This samosa recipe is stuffed with sweet potato dry curry. This samosa filling can also be eaten with rice or naan. You can also add coconut in it and if you like it extra spicy then add some chili powder. Serve with mint chutney.

Servings: 12
Preparation Time: 50 minutes

INGREDIENTS:

- Sweet potato, 2
- Dil leaves, ½ cup
- Garam masala powder, ½ teaspoon
- Salt, to taste
- Green chili, 2, chopped
- Cumin seeds, ½ teaspoon
- Ginger, ½ inch piece grated
- Curry leaves, 6
- Turmeric powder, 1 pinch
- Mustard seeds, ½ teaspoon
- Coriander leaves, 1 tablespoon
- Oil, 1 tablespoon
- Samosa sheets, 12

METHOD:

1. Peel potatoes and cut into small bite size pieces.
2. Chop dil leaves.
3. Temper mustard seeds in 1 tablespoon oil. Add cumin seeds and sauté for 15 minute.
4. Add potatoes and dil leaves. Combine well. Fry the mixture for 2 minutes.
5. Splash ½ cup water and cook over low flame until veggies are tender.
6. Add spices and combine well.
7. When the potatoes are done and the water has dried add coriander leaves and mix well.
8. Now take each samosa sheet and fold the edges to make a cone shape. Stuff the cone with spoonful potato-dil stuffing.
9. Apply a little water on the outer edges to bind well.
10. Deep fry until golden.
11. Serve immediately.

GUJRATI SAMOSA

This is a traditional samosa recipe of Gujrat. The filling is made with potatoes, cabbage, peas and is seasoned with various spices. If you want you can omit onions from the recipe. The quantity of sugar is very moderate therefore these samosas are not very sweet in taste.

Servings: 18
Preparation Time: 35 minutes

INGREDIENT:

- Potatoes, ¾ cup, chopped
- Cabbage, ¾ cup, chopped
- Lemon juice, ½ tablespoon
- Onions, 1/3 cup, chopped
- Green peas, ¾ cup, crushed
- Salt, to taste
- Oil, ¾ tablespoon
- Sugar, ¾ tablespoon
- Coriander, 3 tablespoons, chopped
- Ginger-green chili paste, 1 ½ teaspoon
- Samosa sheets, 18

METHOD:

1. Sauté onions on medium flame until translucent.
2. Add peas and potatoes and cook until potatoes are tender. Stir occasionally.
3. Add a little water if required.
4. Now add cabbage, lemon juice, salt, sugar and ginger-green chili paste. Combine well and cover the lid. Cook for 10 minutes or until the veggies are tender.
5. Add coriander and combine well. Let the filling cool down a little.
6. Take each samosa sheet and fold the edges to form a triangle. Add the filling and fold again in triangular direction and seal by overlapping the remaining edges.
7. Deep fry until golden.
8. Serve immediately.

CURRIED PEAS AND POTATO SAMOSA

This samosa recipe is made with very few ingredients. If you have some lying around in the back of your freezer and some potatoes in the pantry then all you have to do is mix them with a few spices and stuff them in samosa sheets. If you don't have samosa sheets at hand and are too lazy to make some at home then you can also use pie crust.

Servings: 12

Preparation Time: 20 minutes

INGREDIENTS:

- Potatoes, 2 cups, mashed
- Peas, 1 ¼ cups
- Curry powder, 1 ½ teaspoon
- Onion, 1, chopped
- Olive oil, 1 tablespoon
- Black pepper, to taste
- Salt, to taste

METHOD:

1. Sauté onions until translucent.
2. Add peas and potatoes. Season with curry powder, salt and pepper.
3. Combine everything well. Cook for 10 minutes.
4. Take each samosa sheet and fold the edges in a triangular shape. Fill the triangles with potato-pea filling and seal tightly.
5. Deep fry until golden.
6. Serve immediately with mango chutney.

ALLOO SAMOSA

This potato samosa recipe is a relatively spicy version of other potato recipes. You can incorporate carrots and cabbage in it as well if you like. Serve these hot samosas with mint chutney or raita.

Servings: 12

Preparation Time: 30 minutes

INGREDIENTS:

- Potatoes, 3, chopped
- Asafetida, 1 pinch
- Fennel seeds, ½ teaspoon
- Red chili powder, ¼ teaspoon
- Dry pomegranate seeds, 2 teaspoons
- Cumin seeds, ½ teaspoon
- Black pepper, to taste
- Salt, to taste
- Ground coriander seeds, 1 teaspoon
- Green peas, 1 cup
- Ground cinnamon, ¼ inch
- Ground green cardamom, 1
- Green chili, 1, chopped
- Ginger, ½ inch, crushed
- Clove, 1

METHOD:

1. Temper cumin seeds and ginger. Add peas and potatoes. Fry for 2 minutes.
2. Add all the seasoning spices and combine well.
3. Cook until the potatoes are tender.
4. Take each samosa sheet and form a cone shape. Fill the cone with spicy potato filling and seal.
5. Deep fry until golden.
6. Serve immediately.

TURKEY SAMOSA

If you do not have unseasoned turkey meat then you can also use some leftover cooked and seasoned turkey that has been waiting in the freezer for a while. Serve these crispy and crunchy samosas with mint chutney, mango chutney or tamarind chutney.

Servings: 6-8
Preparation Time: 25 minutes

INGREDIENTS:

- Turkey, 3 cups, cooked
- Unsalted butter, 4 tablespoons
- Green beans, ½ cup, diced
- Garlic, 4 cloves, minced
- Yellow onion, ½, chopped
- Hot red chilies, 2, sliced
- Mashed potatoes, 1 cup
- Brown mustard seeds, 1 teaspoon
- Curry powder, ½ teaspoon
- Salt, to taste
- Garam masala, 1 teaspoon
- Cumin seeds, ½ teaspoon

METHOD:

1. Melt butter and add onions. Season with garam masala, curry powder, mustard and cumin seeds. Sauté for 3 minutes.
2. Add garlic and sauté until the garlic infuses its aroma.
3. Remove pan off the flame and add the remaining ingredients. Combine everything well.
4. Now take each samosa filling and fold the edges to form a triangle. Fill the triangle with the stuffing and seal tightly.
5. Deep fry until golden.
6. Serve immediately.

CHICKEN AND SPINACH SAMOSA

Spinach is high in magnesium and makes a delicious filling for various recipes. These chicken and spinach samosas are great in taste. Serve them with mint raita or tomato sauce for extra flavor.

Servings: 8

Preparation Time: 30 minutes

INGREDIENTS:

- Ground chicken, 1 pound
- Spinach, 1 cup
- Ground cumin, 2 teaspoons
- Salt, to taste
- Black pepper, to taste
- Onion, 1 small, chopped
- Ground red chili powder, 2 teaspoons
- Chickpeas, 1 can, cooked
- Cinnamon, ½ teaspoon
- Curry powder, 4 tablespoons
- Ginger, 2 teaspoons, minced
- Garlic, 2 cloves, minced

METHOD:

1. Heat vegetable oil in a pan. Temper all the spices until aromatic.
2. Add chicken and cook until slightly brown.
3. Now add onions, spinach, ginger, garlic, salt, pepper and chickpeas. Combine well.
4. Simmer for 15 minutes.
5. Take each samosa sheet and fold the corner to make a triangle. Fill the triangle with the spinach-chicken mixture.
6. Apply a little water over the open edges of the samosa sheet to seal.
7. Deep fry until golden.
8. Serve immediately.

PALAK PANEER SAMOSA

This is another spinach recipe but this time with the addition of paneer. Paneer is used in various Indian cuisines and has been a traditional ingredient of decades. These samosas can be served with coriander and mint chutney or red chili sauce.

Servings: 8-10

Preparation Time: 25 minutes

INGREDIENTS:

- Spinach, 1bunch, blanched and chopped
- Yogurt, 1 tablespoon
- Green chilies, 3, chopped
- Cumin powder, ½ teaspoon
- Tomato, ½, chopped
- Cheddar cheese, 4 cubes, chopped
- Pepper powder, ½ teaspoon
- Ginger-garlic paste, 1 tablespoon
- Turmeric powder, ½ teaspoon
- Coriander powder, ½ teaspoon
- Paneer, 50 g, crumbled
- Onion, ½, chopped
- Garam masala, ½ teaspoon
- Chili powder, ½ teaspoon

METHOD:

1. Temper ginger-garlic paste in ghee or oil until fragrant.
2. Add onion and sauté for 2 minutes.
3. Add tomatoes and chili powder and cook for 3-5 minutes.
4. Add the spices and fry for 3 minutes.
5. Now add yogurt and cook for another 3 minutes. Add spinach and fry for a few minutes.
6. Add paneer and season with salt. Cook for 5 minutes.
7. Remove the mixture from heat and add cheese. Combine everything well and let the cheese melt.
8. Take samosa sheets and fold the edges to form a triangle. Fill the triangle with the filling and seal tightly.
9. Deep fry until golden.
10. Serve immediately.

CURRIED SHRIMP SAMOSA

Shrimps are my all-time favorite and I am always looking around for recipes that use shrimps. This shrimp filling is simply delicious. The ingredients used are easily available in your pantry. Serve these samosa bites with mint chutney or chili sauce.

Servings: 8
Preparation Time: 20 minutes

INGREDIENTS:

- Shrimp, 8 oz. peeled , deveined and tails removed
- Egg, ¼ cup
- Basil, 2 tablespoon, chopped
- Green onion, 2 bunches, chopped
- Curry powder, ½ teaspoon
- Ginger paste, ½ teaspoon
- Salt, to taste
- Samosa sheets, 8

METHOD:

1. Finely chop shrimps and keep aside.
2. Tender-fry green onions and add shrimps. Combine well.
3. Season with salt and curry powder. Cook for 5 minutes.
4. Now add basil and combine everything.
5. Take each samosa sheet and fold the corners to form a cone shape. Stuff the cones with shrimp mixture and seal tightly.
6. Deep fry until golden.
7. Serve immediately.

BEEF LENTIL SAMOSA

Beef and lentils are a great combination for samosa stuffing. You can also use canned lentils in this recipe. If you are not using canned lentils then soak the lentils for 30 minutes at least prior to cooking. Serve samosas with mint raita or tamarind chutney.

Servings: 24
Preparation Time: 20 minutes

INGREDIENTS:

- Lean ground beef, ½ pound
- Green lentils, 1 cup, cooked
- Cilantro, ½ cup, chopped
- Jalapeno pepper, 1, chopped
- Black pepper, ½ teaspoon
- Salt, ½ teaspoon
- Garlic, 2 cloves, minced
- Cumin, 1 teaspoon
- Green onions, 2, chopped
- Onion, 1, chopped
- Ginger, 2 teaspoon, grated
- Garam masala, ½ teaspoon

METHOD:

1. Sauté onions for 6 minutes and add beef. Cook until beef changes its color.
2. Add garlic, jalapeno, lentils and ginger. Combine everything and cook for 3 minutes.
3. Now season with all the spices and garnish with cilantro. Mix well to incorporate.
4. Take each samosa sheet and fold the corner to make a triangle, fill each triangle with beef filling and seal tightly.
5. Deep fry until golden.
6. Serve immediately.

PORK SAMOSA

Want to try out something new with pork meat? Try this pork samosa filling mixed with vegetables and seasoned with curry powder. It is ideal to serve with hot red chili sauce or tomato sauce.

Servings: 20
Preparation Time: 20 minutes

INGREDIENTS:

- Lean ground pork, ½ pound
- Carrot, 1, chopped
- Peas, ¼ cup
- Onion,1 chopped
- Potato, 2, chopped
- Butter, 2 tablespoon
- Curry paste, 2 tablespoon
- Salt, to taste
- Pepper, to taste

METHOD:

1. Sauté pork with onions and brown and fragrant.
2. Stir curry paste and cook for 5 minutes.
3. Add carrots, potato and peas. Mix all the seasoning and cook 5 minutes.
4. Take each samosa sheet and fold to make triangle. Stuff each triangle with pork filling and seal tightly.
5. Deep fry until golden.
6. Serve immediately.

TANDOORI CHICKEN SAMOSA

Tandoori chicken is a hot favorite not only in the Subcontinent, but also across the world. Known for its spicy flavor, it is an ideal item to serve for dinner. If you want to add a new twist to this type of chicken, try wrapping tandoori chicken meat in a samosa.

Servings: 12

Preparation Time: 30 minutes

INGREDIENTS:

- Tandoori curry paste, 1 tablespoon
- Garam masala, 2 teaspoon
- Potatoes, 2, cooked and coarsely chopped
- Green chili, 1, chopped
- Yogurt, 1 tablespoon
- Peas, 1 cup
- Chicken breasts, 2,
- Lemon juice, 1 teaspoon
- Black mustard seeds, 1 teaspoon
- Ground turmeric, ½ teaspoon
- Onion, 1, chopped
- Curry leaves, 10, chopped
- Coriander leaves, 2 tablespoon
- Black pepper, ½ teaspoon
- Garlic, 4 cloves, crushed
- Salt, to taste

METHOD:

1. Preheat the oven to 350F.
2. Mix tandoori paste and yogurt together. Whisk until no lumps remain. Coat chicken in this mixture evenly and let it stand for 60 minutes in freezer.
3. Bake chicken for 20 minutes or until done. Chop the chicken to form mince like texture.
4. Sauté onions for 3 minutes and add turmeric, mustard seeds, salt, garam masala and pepper. Cook for 1 minute.
5. Add chilies, curry leaves and garlic and fry for 5 minutes. Now add peas and potatoes and cover the lid. Cook for 10 minutes.
6. Now add chicken cubes and lemon juice. Sprinkle coriander leaves and combine everything well.

7. Take each samosa sheet and fold to make a triangle. Fill the triangle with the stuffing and seal tightly.
8. Deep fry until golden.
9. Serve immediately.

CAULIFLOWER AND BROCCOLI SAMOSA

I personally don't prefer eating broccoli on its own, but this filling mixture is super tasty. Mixed with cauliflower and shallots these samosa bites gives a cheesy texture in every bite. To be served with tomato sauce or coriander chutney.

Photo Credit: Flickr User Okayryan,
<https://www.flickr.com/photos/24219366@N06/6205347632>

Servings:	20
Preparation Time:	20 minutes

INGREDIENTS:

- Broccoli florets, 8 oz.
- Cauliflower florets, 8 oz.
- Mozzarella, 4 oz. diced
- Curry powder, 1 tablespoon
- Vegetable stock, 2 tablespoon
- Shallots, 3, chopped
- Tomatoes, 2, chopped
- Egg yolk, 1
- Poppy seeds, 2 tablespoons
- Mint, 1 tablespoon, chopped
- Double cream, 1 tablespoon
- Flour, 1 teaspoon
- Salt, to taste
- Pepper, to taste

METHOD:

1. Cook shallots and florets for 5 minutes.
2. Add all the seasoning spices and combine well. Cook for 3 minutes.
3. Now add tomatoes, stock and water. Cover the lid and cook for 5 minutes over low flame.
4. Remove from flame and add mint and mozzarella. Combine together to incorporate.
5. Take each samosa sheet and fold the ends to form a triangle. Stuff the filling and seal tightly.
6. Deep fry until golden.
7. Serve immediately.

PUMPKIN SAMOSA

It's pumpkin harvesting season and there are pumpkins everywhere. Nothing tastes better than cooking fresh pumpkin. This filling is made from fresh pumpkin toasted in olive oil for a caramelized texture. Plan to serve it with mango chutney.

Photo Credit: Flickr user Krista,
<https://www.flickr.com/photos/scaredykat/7797164800>

Servings: 20

Preparation Time: 20 minutes

INGREDIENTS:

- Sugar pie pumpkin, 2 cups, diced and seasoned with salt and a few drops of oil and toasted until caramelized
- Curry powder, 2 teaspoon
- Yellow onion, 1, chopped
- Ground turmeric, ½ teaspoon
- Ginger, 2 teaspoon
- Jalapeno pepper, 1, roasted and chopped
- Lemon juice, 2 teaspoon
- Peas, ½ cup

METHOD:

1. Sauté onions for 3 minutes. Add jalapeno, turmeric, ginger and curry powder. Mix well and fry for 40 seconds.
2. Add pumpkin and combine with the spices well. Add peas and stir again.
3. Stir lemon juice and cover the lid. Cook for 5 minutes.
4. Take each samosa sheet and fold the edges to form a triangle. Fill the triangle with pumpkin mixture and seal tightly.
5. Deep fry until golden.
6. Serve immediately.

ARTICHOKE SAMOSA

Artichoke and chickpea filling is actually a complete meal that can be served with rice or tortillas. This recipe makes more than a dozen samosas that you can freeze for weeks. Serve hot with green chutney.

Servings:	14-18
Preparation Time:	30 minutes

INGREDIENTS:

- Artichoke hearts, 1, halved
- Chickpeas, 1 can, rinsed
- Red onion, 1 large, chopped
- Turmeric, ¼ teaspoon
- Cumin seeds, 1 teaspoon
- Yogurt, 3 tablespoon, whisked
- Garam masala, ½ teaspoon
- Ginger-garlic paste, 2 tablespoon
- Salt, to taste
- Paprika, ¼ teaspoon
- Coriander, 2 teaspoon
- Roma tomatoes, 3, chopped
- Lime juice, 2 tablespoon
- Coriander leaves, 2 tablespoon

METHOD:

1. Grind onion, tomatoes and garlic paste in a food processor until a thick paste if formed.
2. Temper cumin seeds and add puree. Sauté for 10 minutes or until thick and dark.
3. Add all the spices and mix. Add yogurt gradually while stirring continuously.
4. Lastly add artichokes, lime juice and chickpeas. Combine well. Cover the lid and simmer on low for 15 minutes.
5. Take each samosa sheet and fold the edges to form a cone shape.
6. Fill the cones with the mixture and apply a little water on the open edge to bind.
7. Deep fry until golden.
8. Serve immediately.

EGGPLANT SAMOSA

I personally like the color of eggplants a lot. It is so refreshing and lively to the eyes. You can also chop up the eggplants and cook them with spices and stuff them in samosa sheets. Grilling gives eggplants enhanced flavor.

Servings: 12

Preparation Time: 20 minutes

INGREDIENTS:

- Grilled eggplant, 2 cups
- Cumin seeds, ½ teaspoon
- Salt, to taste
- Pepper, to taste
- Parmesan cheese, 1 cup, grated
- Garlic, 1 clove, minced
- Parsley, 2 teaspoon

METHOD:

1. Preheat the oven to 350 F.
2. Slightly slit the eggplant lengthwise and stuff with garlic, salt and pepper. Add a few drops of oil. Enclose the eggplant tightly and wrap it in foil. Roast in the oven for 30 minutes.
3. Combine the entire ingredients make a smooth puree. Drain excess oil.
4. Take each samosa sheet and fold the ends to make a cone shape. Stuff the cone with eggplant mixture and enclose the ends tightly.
5. Deep fry until golden.
6. Serve immediately.

CONCLUSION

Cooking samosas at home has gained much popularity in recent years and has become every household's common dish. Served with green chutney, raita, mango chutney and red chili chutney, samosas have become the heart of dinners, snacks and made their way to lunch boxes. Be it chicken filled or beef filled or veggie filled, every flavor is mouthwatering to the very end.

This cookbook contains 30 easy to make samosa recipes, giving you diversity in fillings to choose from. This cookbook contains recipes mostly from India, giving you a chance to sneak your way to the samosa realm.

The recipes featured in this samosa cookbook contain paneer, mozzarella, potato, peas, fish, shrimp and some very basic spices. We have put together all the healthy ingredients in these fillings, especially those vegetables that are not every famous among children, for example broccoli, spinach and eggplant.

If you want to save time and don't like standing in front of the stove for too long, then you can also oven bake the samosas. The method and ingredients will remain the same, just the deep frying will be replaced by baking. Normally samosas take 30-35 minutes to bake on 350 F.

The exciting thing about samosas is that they are a great way to accommodate leftovers. Most of us don't like eating the same dish the very next day and throwing it away is like throwing away your hard work, patience and time. So the best way is to keep samosa sheets in your pantry all the time and fill them in and make a whole new samosa version of your own.

Printed in Great Britain
by Amazon